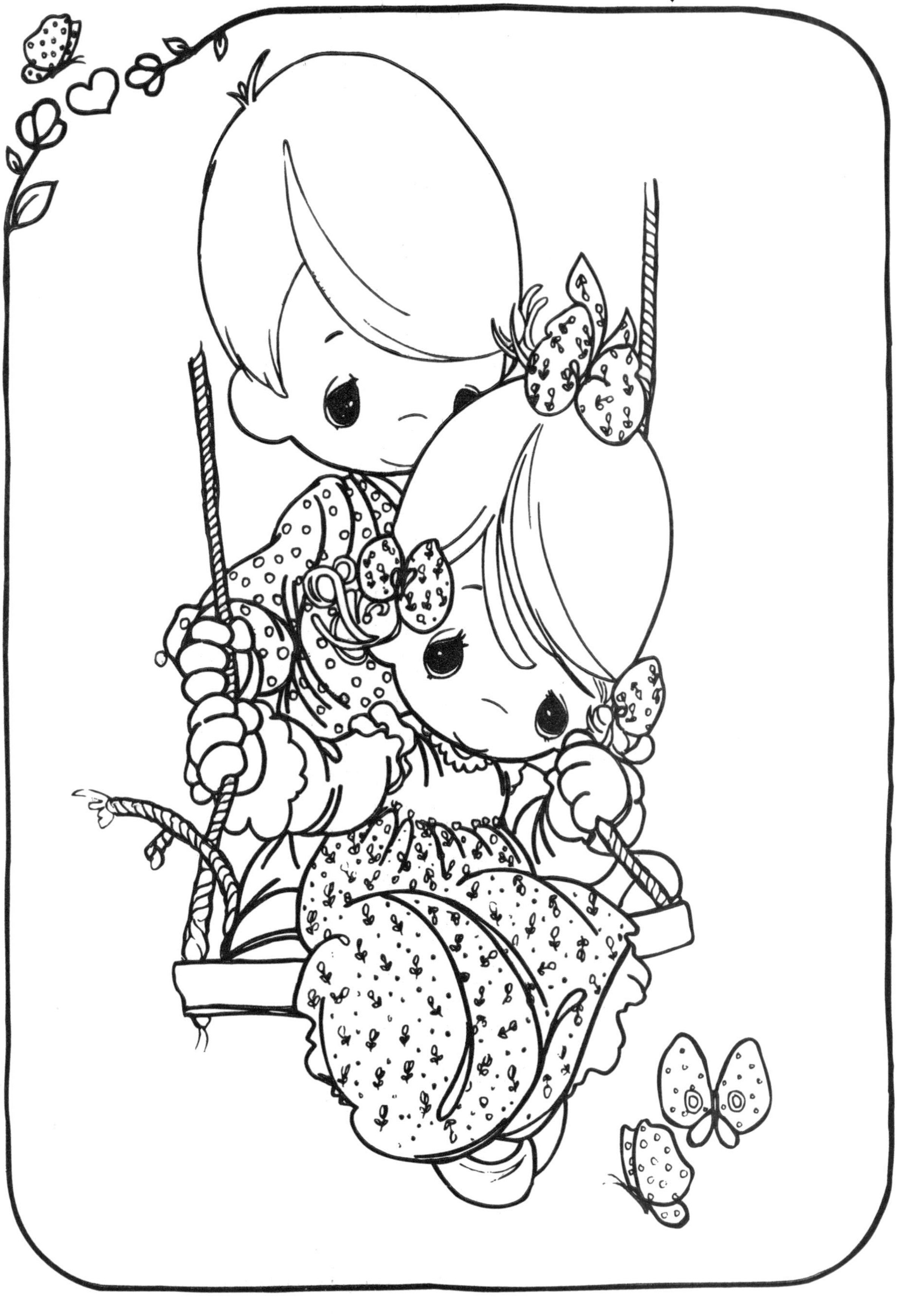

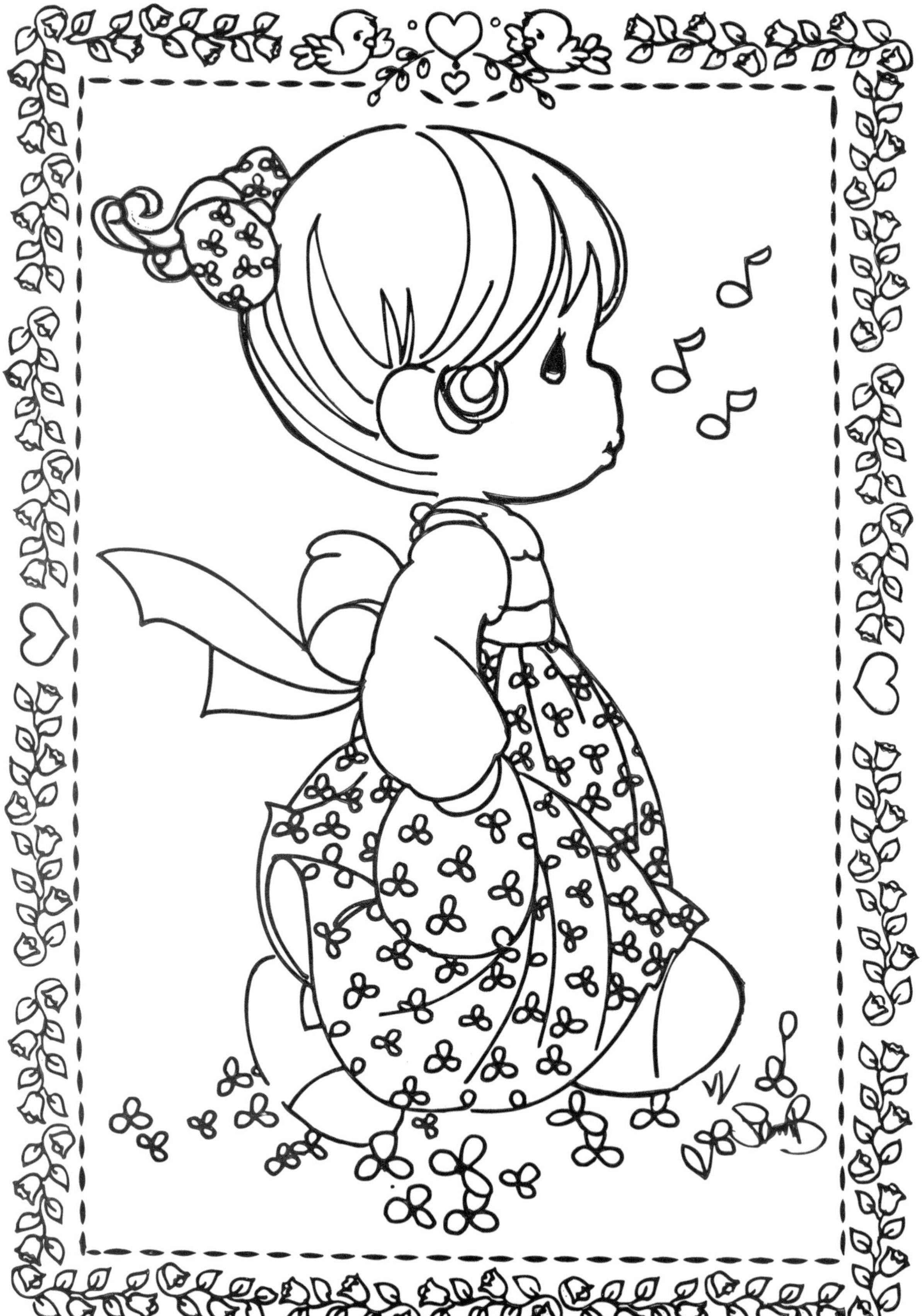

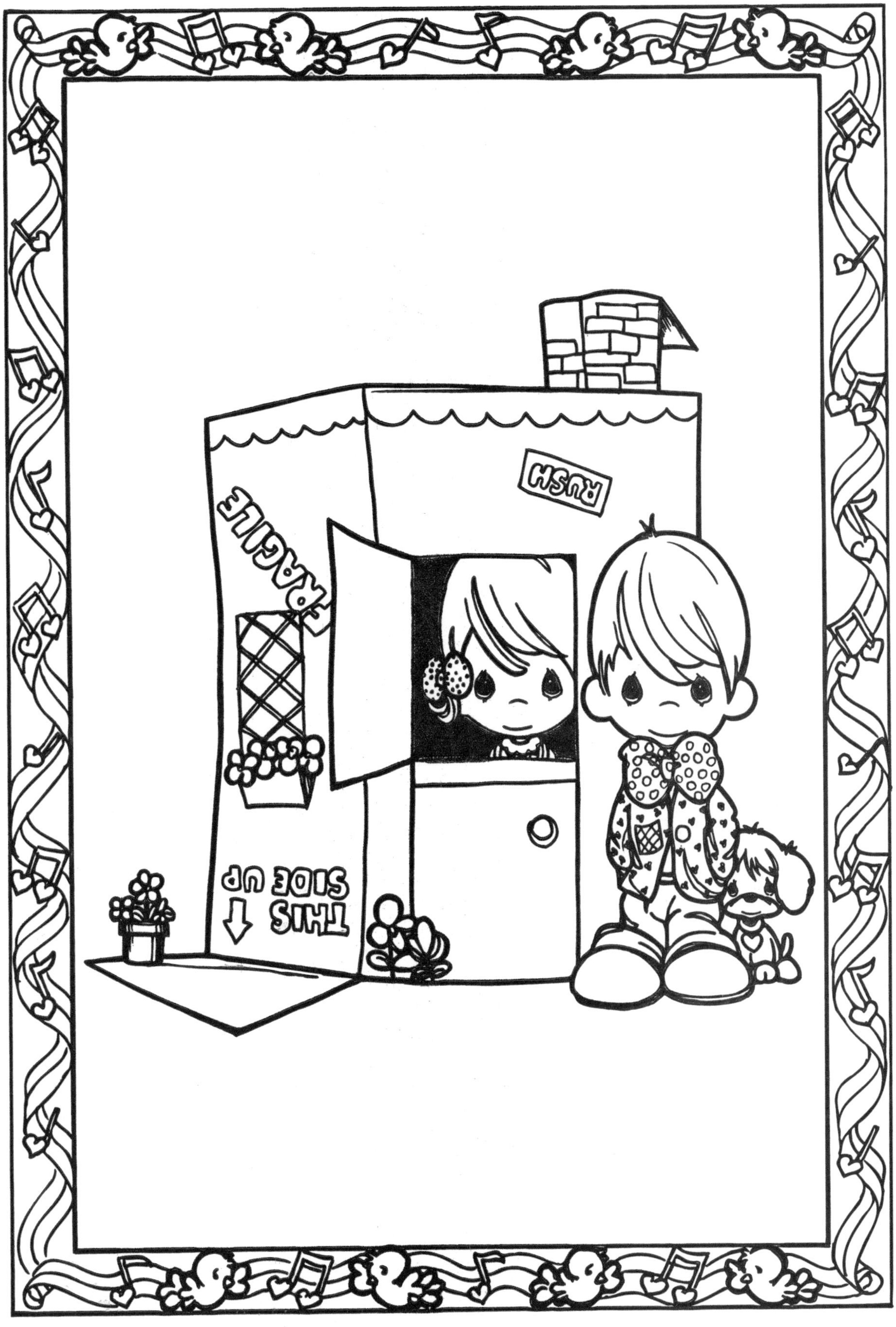
RUSH
THIS SIDE UP

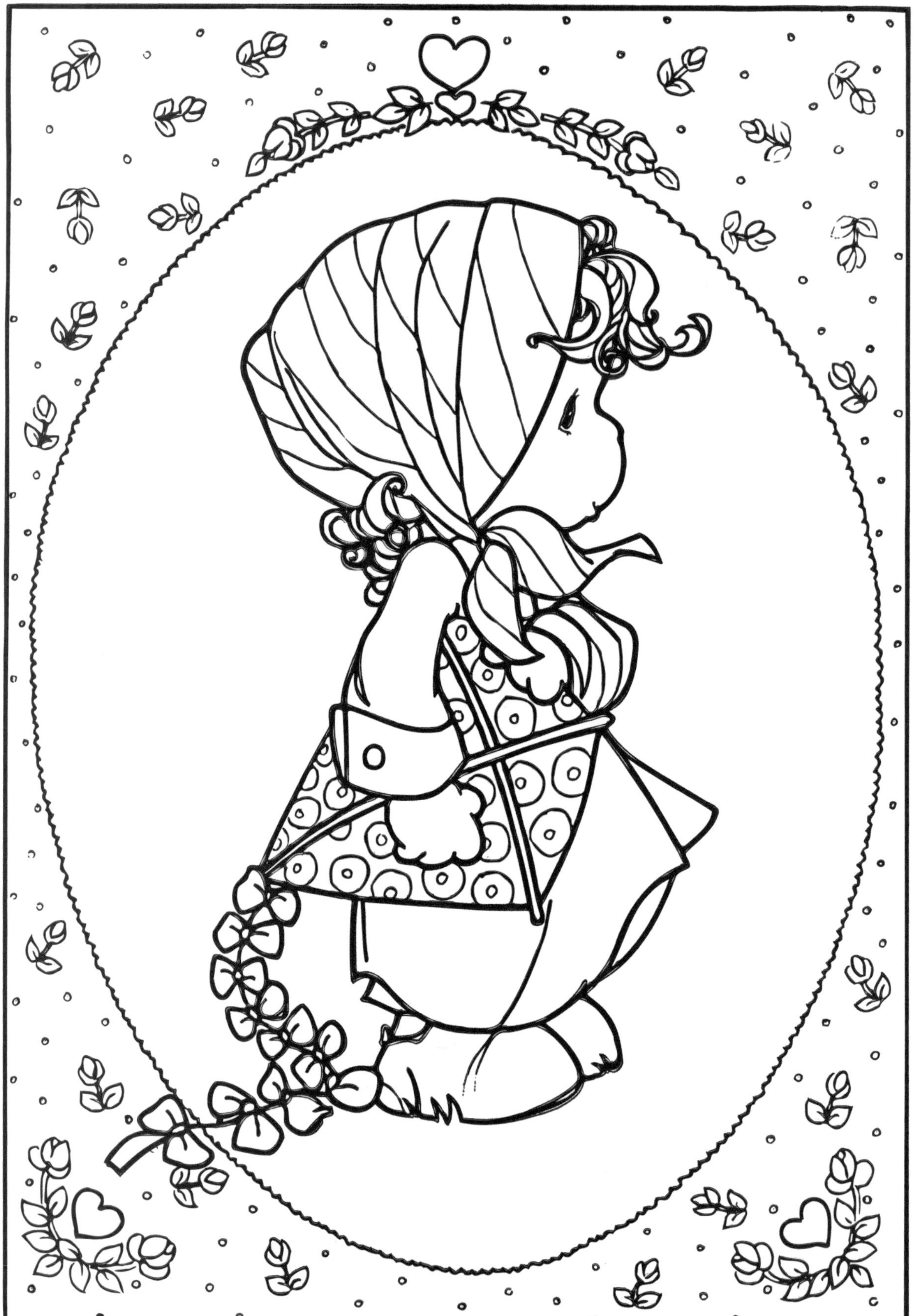

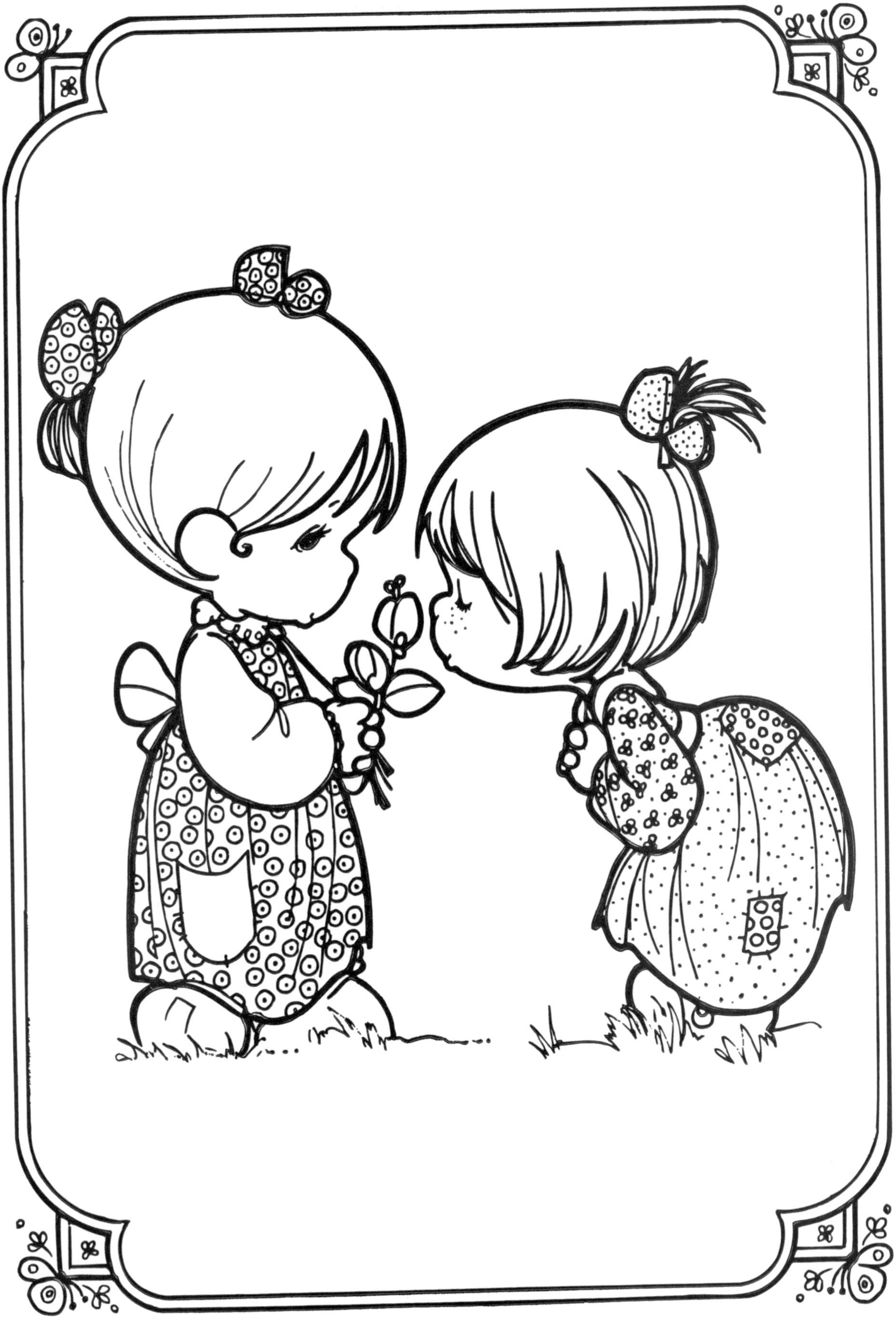

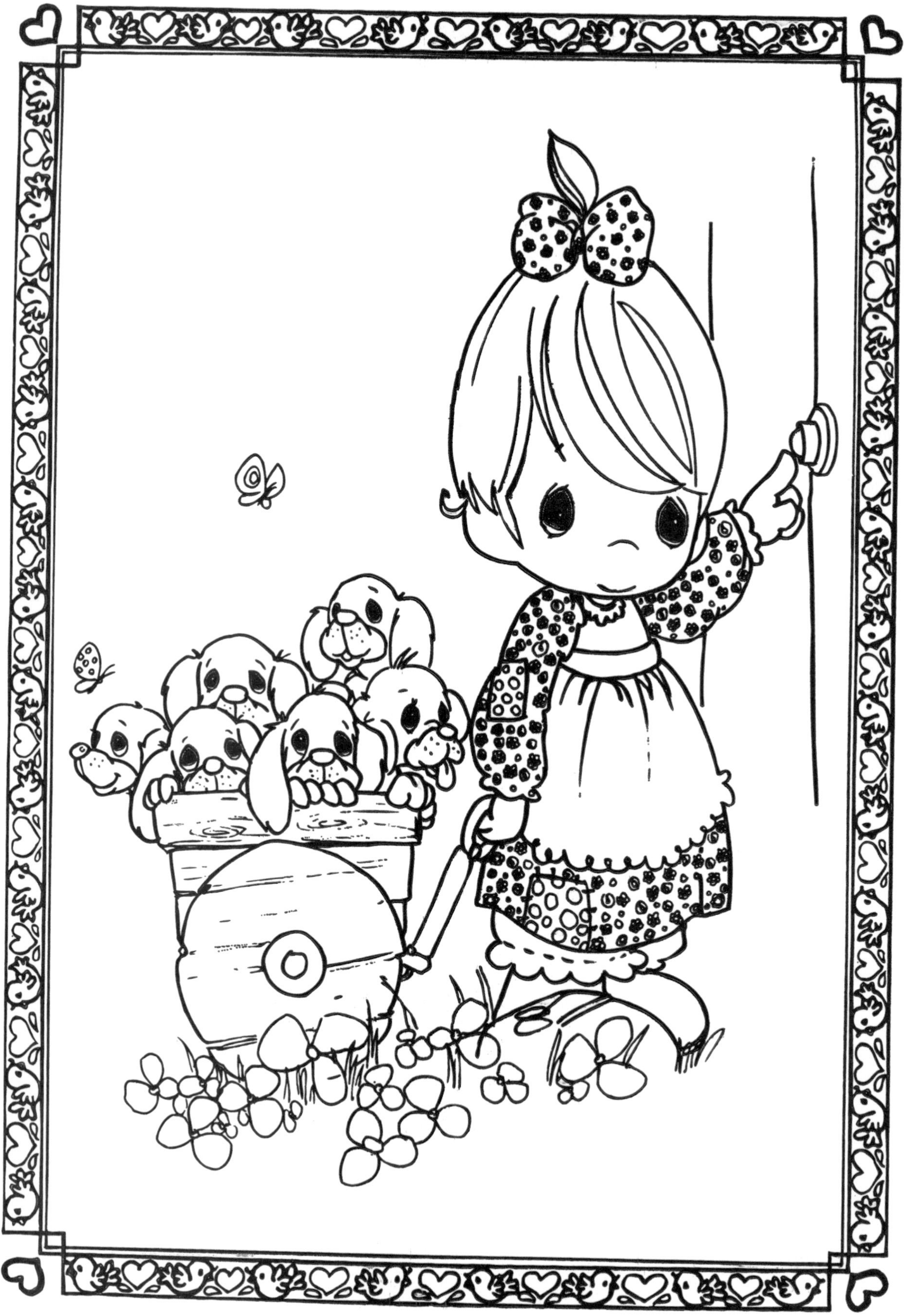

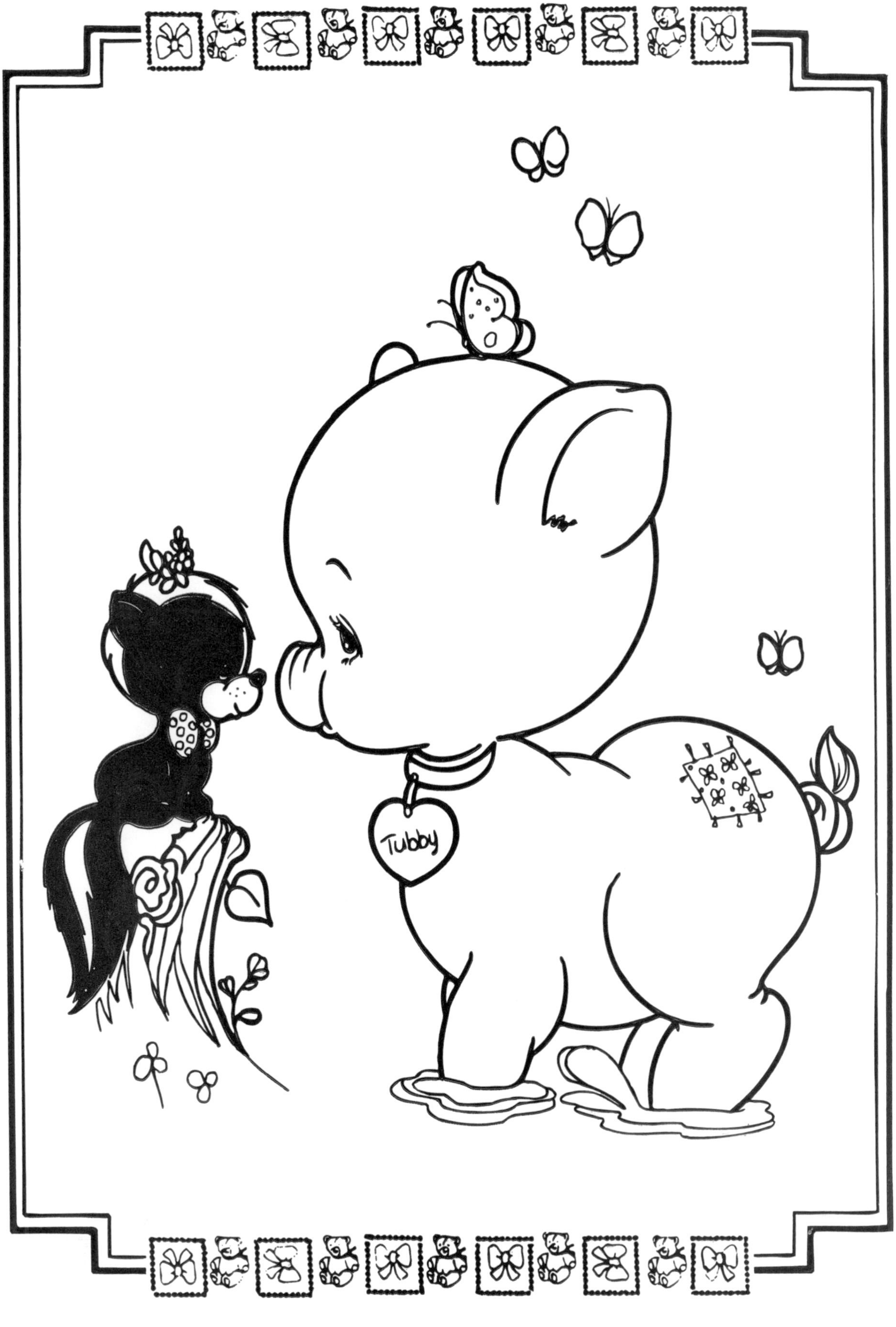
Tubby

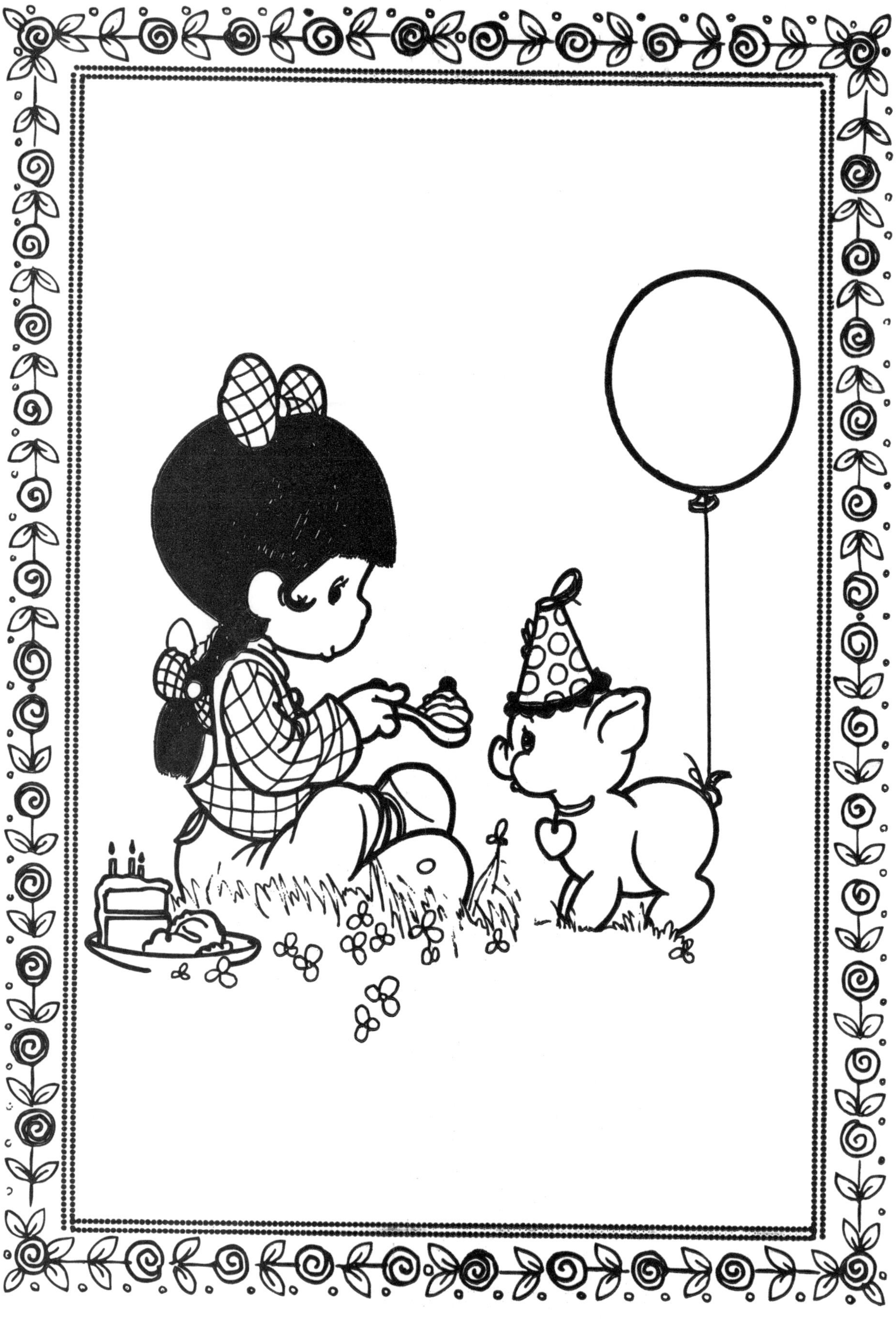

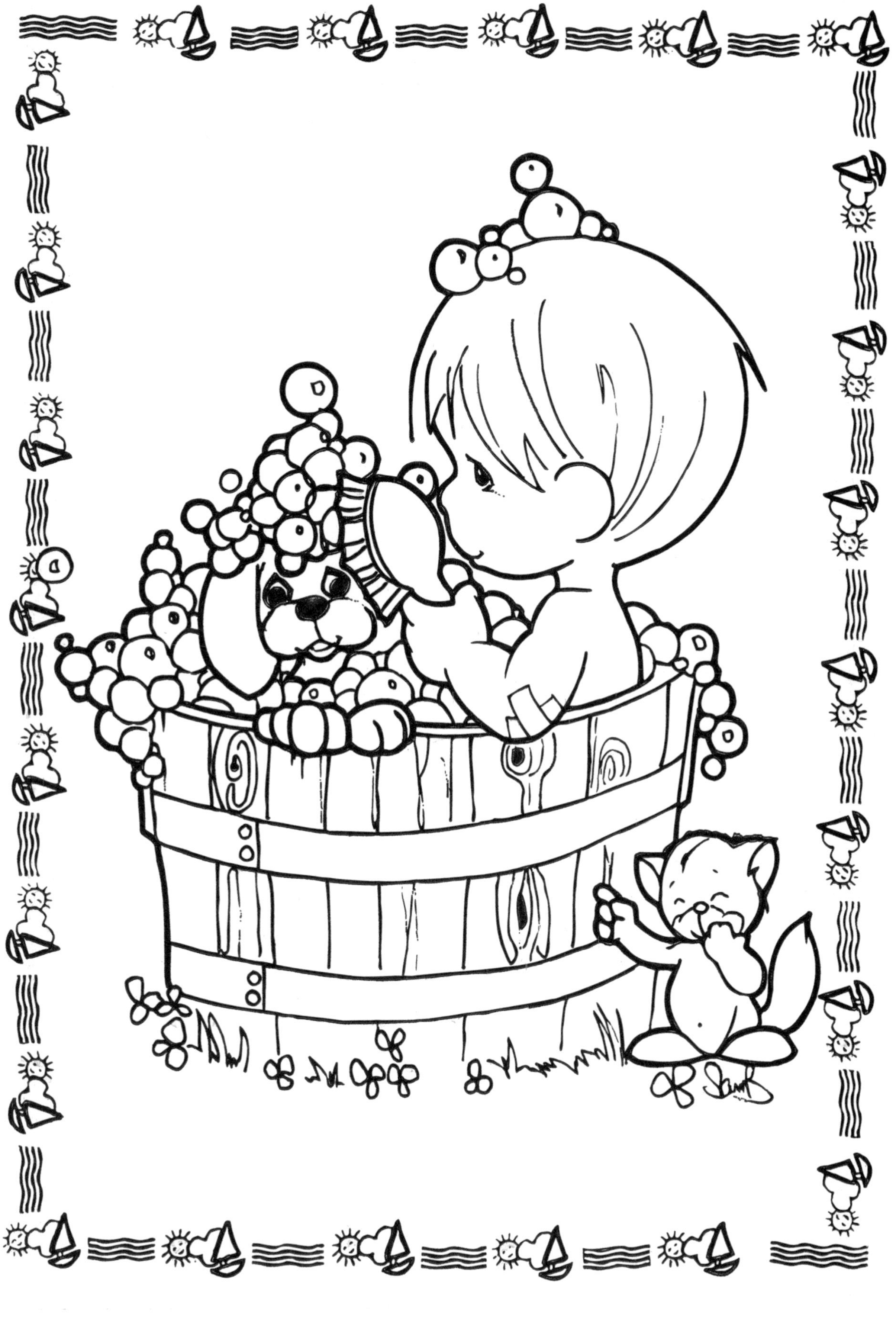

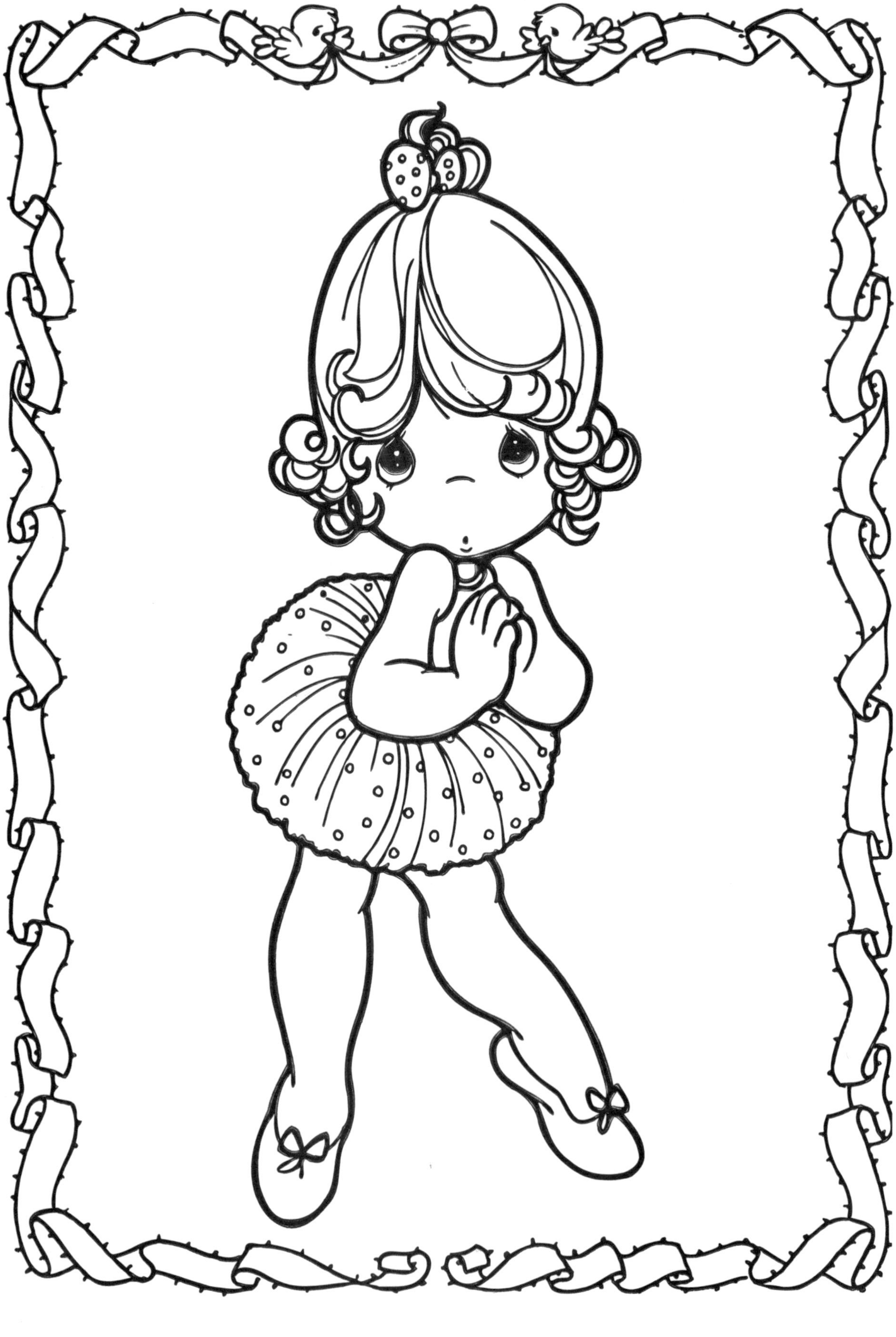

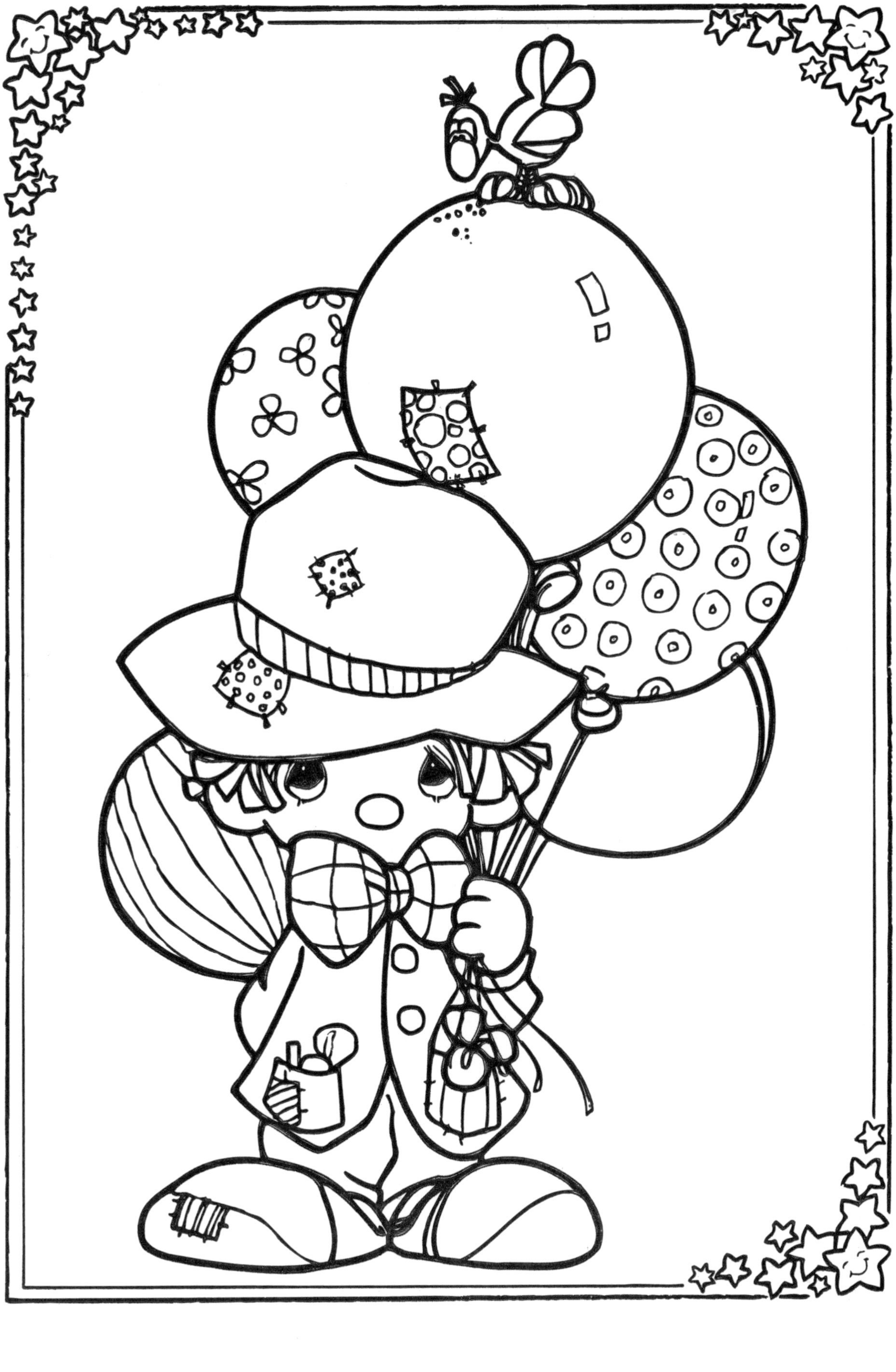

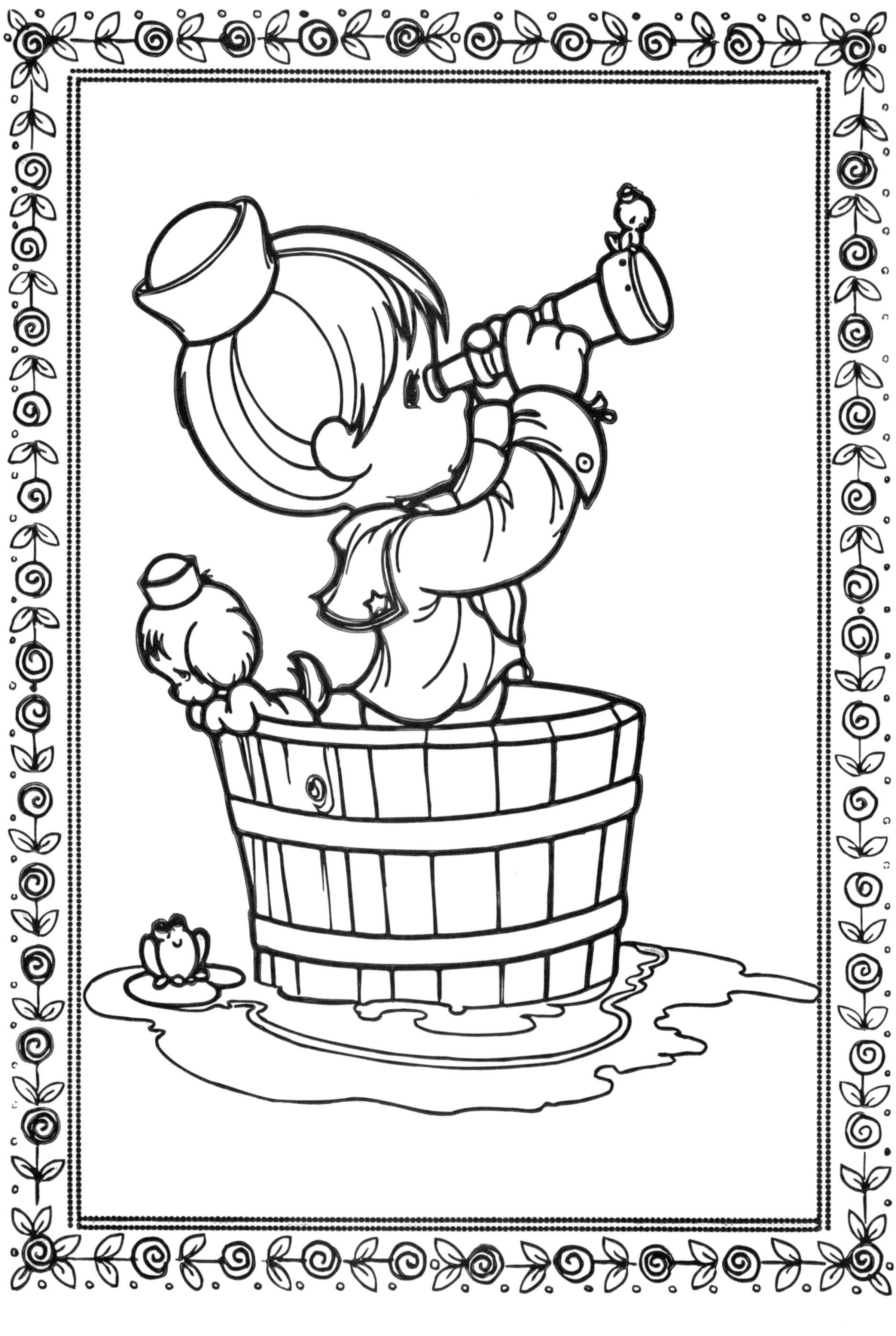

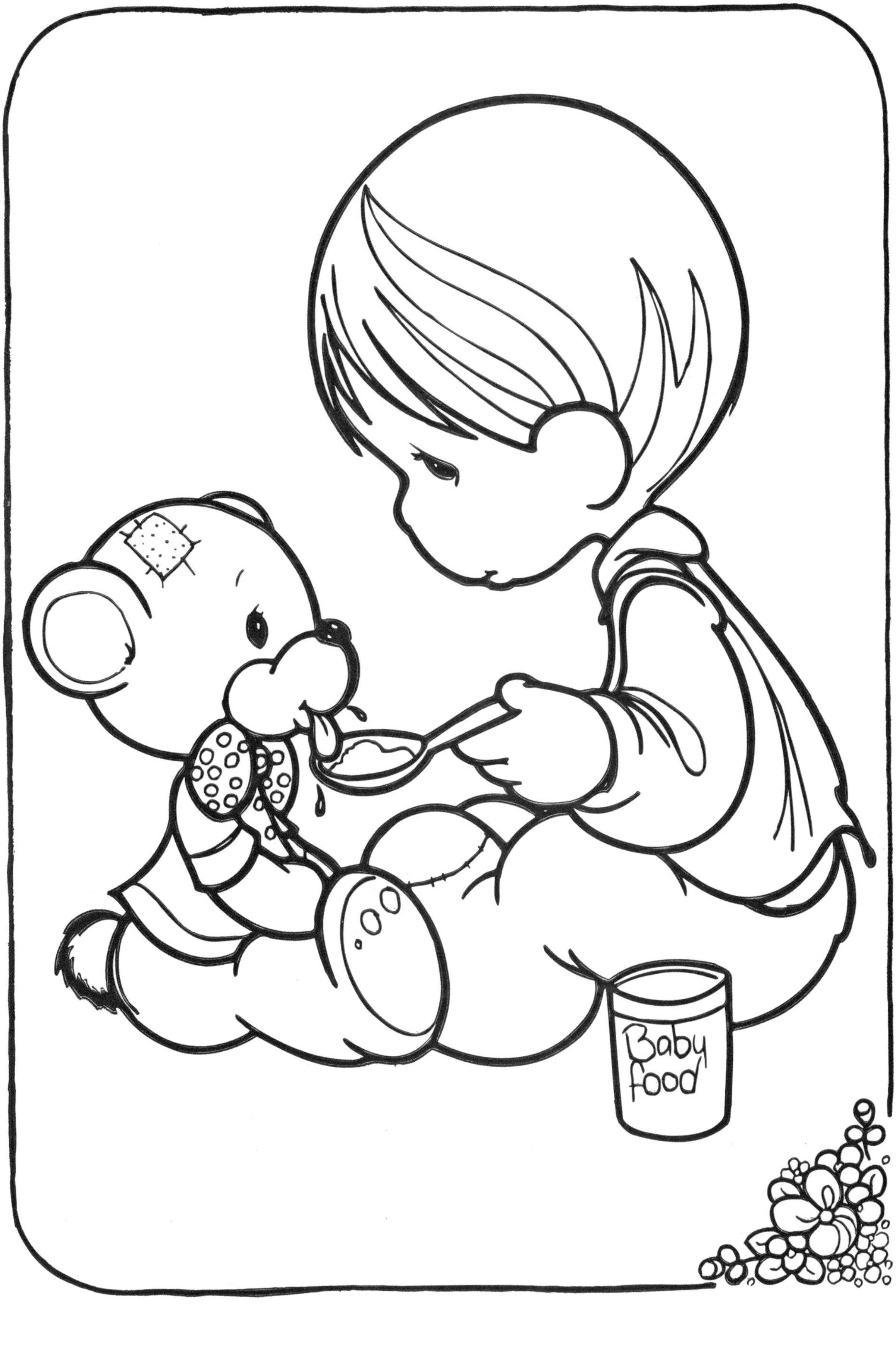
Baby food

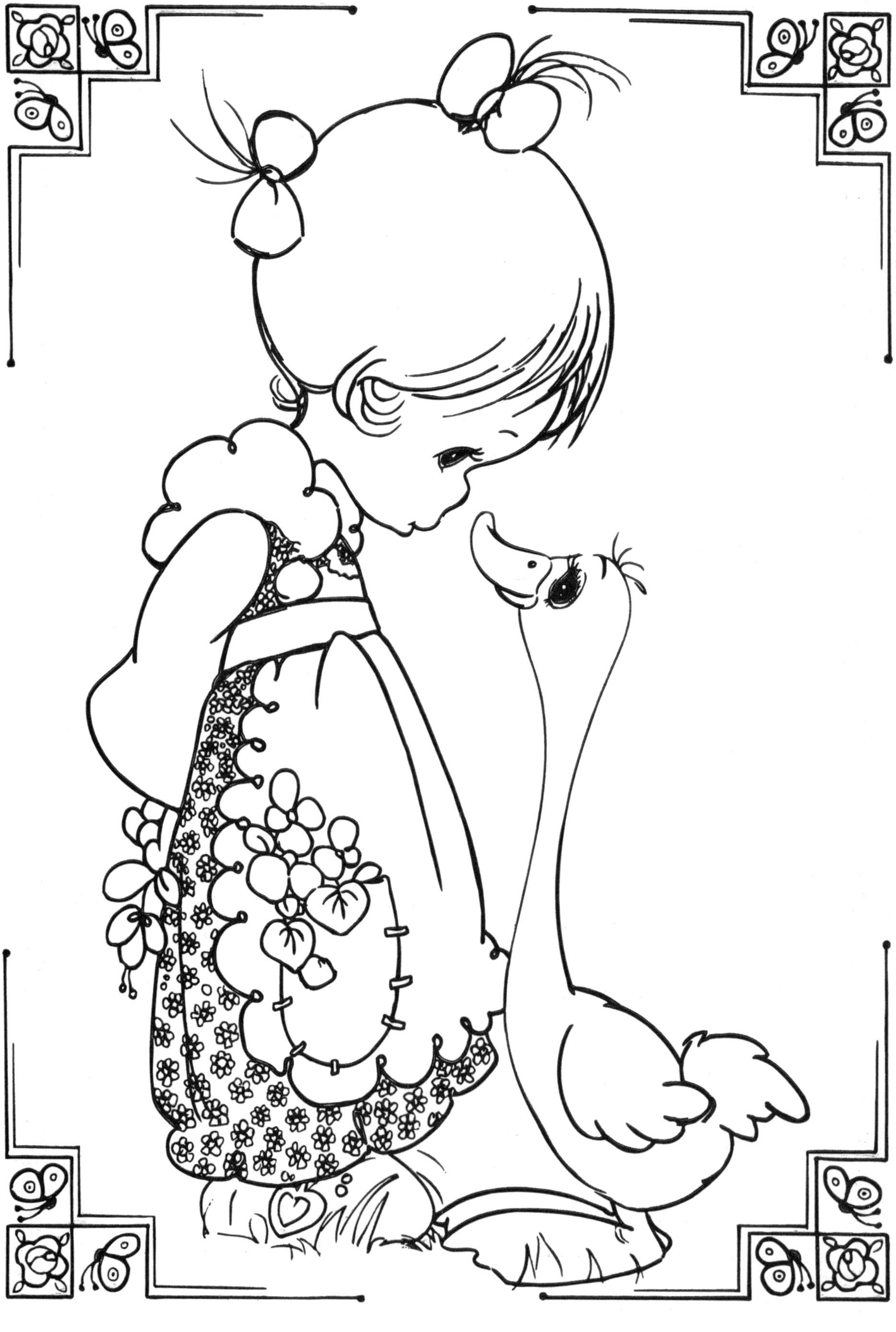

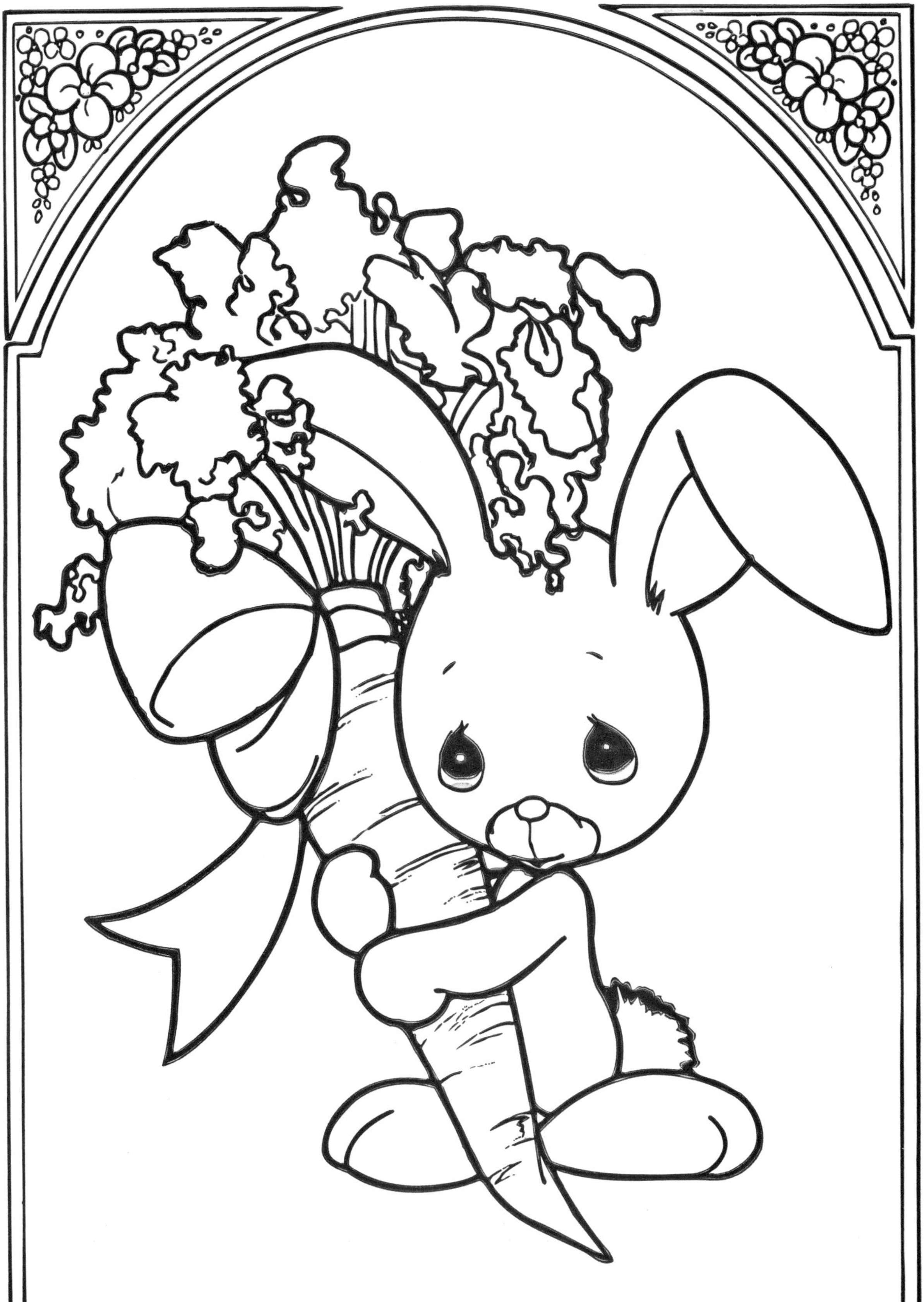

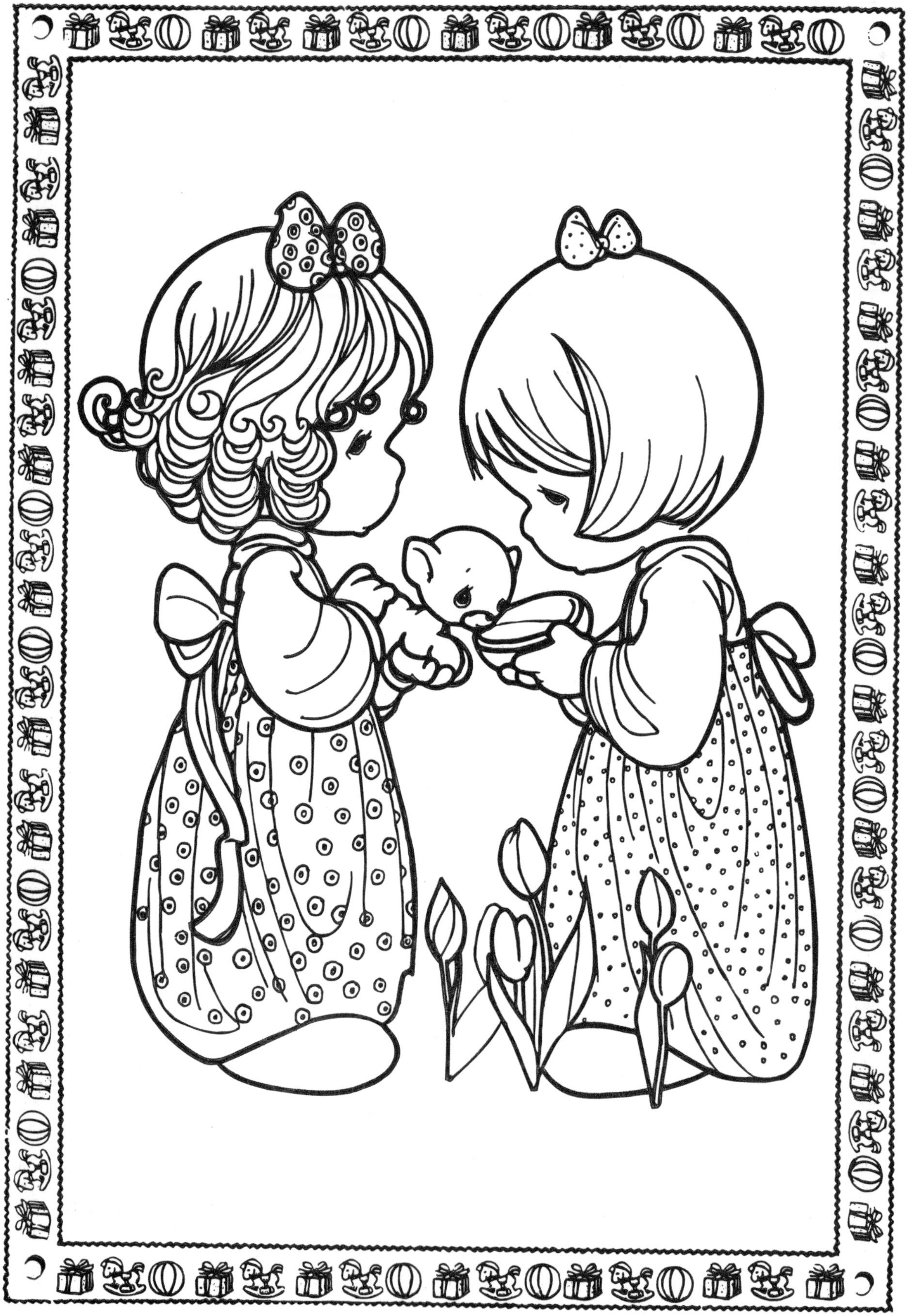